LITTLE BLACK BOOK

A LIGHT SHINES IN THE DARKNESS

BY CURTIS MICHAEL GRAY

EVERYONE KNOWS THE WORLD IS A DARK PLACE. THERE'S A LIGHT THAT SHINES IN THE DARKNESS, BUT THE DARKNESS DOESN'T COMPREHEND IT...

THERE ARE SOME VERY IMPORTANT THINGS EVERYONE SHOULD KNOW: IT WOULD BE A TERRIBLE SHAME IF YOU, AND THE PEOPLE YOU LOVE AND CHERISH, NEVER HAD ANYONE TELL YOU HOW TO NAVIGATE THE DARKNESS OF THIS WORLD. HOPEFULLY, YOU CONTINUE TO READ AND FOR ALL ETERNITY LOOK BACK AT THESE MOMENTS AND THANK GOD FOR HIS GOODNESS AND MERCY. BE HUMBLE AND ASK,

GOD, PLEASE OPEN MY EYES!

BE HUMBLE...

Matthew 18:3-4
Assuredly, I say to you, unless you are converted and become as little children, you will by no means enter the kingdom of heaven. Therefore, whoever humbles himself as this little child is the greatest in the kingdom of heaven.

HUMILITY IS KEY...

James 4:6
God resists the proud, but gives grace to the humble.

James 4:10
Humble yourselves in the sight of the Lord, and He will lift you up.

CLOTHED WITH HUMILITY…

1 Peter 5:5-6
Be clothed with humility, for "God resists the proud, but gives grace to the humble." Therefore, humble yourselves under the mighty hand of God, that He may exalt you in due time.

DARKNESS COVERED EVERYTHING...

Genesis 1:1-3
"In the beginning God created the heavens and the earth. The earth was without form, and void; and darkness was on the face of the deep. And the Spirit of God was hovering over the face of the waters. Then God said, "Let there be light"; and there was light.

JESUS IS THE LIGHT…

John 1:1-5
In the beginning was the Word, and the Word was with God, and the Word was God. He was in the beginning with God. All things were made through Him, and without Him nothing was made that was made. In Him was life, and the life was the light of men. And the light shines in the darkness, and the darkness did not comprehend it.

JESUS CAME TO SAVE US...

John 3:16-18
This is how God loved the world: He gave his one and only Son (Jesus), so that everyone who believes in him will not perish but have eternal life. God sent his Son into the world not to judge the world, but to save the world through him. There is no judgment against anyone who believes in him. But anyone who does not believe in him has already been judged for not believing in God's one and only Son (Jesus).

CALL ON JESUS...

Acts 2:21 NLT
Everyone who calls on the name of the Lord will be saved.

ALL HAVE SINNED...

Rom 3:23
All have sinned and fall short of the glory of God.

WHO COULD SURVIVE?

Psalms 130:3-5
Lord, if you kept a record of our sins, who, O Lord, could ever survive? But you offer forgiveness, that we might learn to fear you. I am counting on the Lord; yes, I am counting on him. I have put my hope in his word.

FORGIVE OTHERS...

Matthew 6:14-15
If you forgive those who sin against you, your heavenly Father will forgive you. But if you refuse to forgive others, your heavenly Father will not forgive your sins.

CONFESS & BE CLEANSED...

1 John 1:9
If we confess our sins to him, he is faithful and just to forgive us our sins and to cleanse us from all wickedness.

NOTHING CAN SEPARATE YOU FROM THE LOVE OF GOD...

Romans 8:38-39
I am convinced that nothing can ever separate us from God's love. Neither death nor life, neither angels nor demons, neither our fears for today nor our worries about tomorrow—not even the powers of hell can separate us from God's love. No power in the sky above or in the earth below—indeed, nothing in all creation will ever be able to separate us from the love of God that is revealed in Christ Jesus our Lord.

JESUS WILL NEVER LEAVE YOU...

Heb 13:5
I will never leave you nor forsake you.

Matt 28:20
I am with you always, even to the end of the age.

GOD IS CALLING YOU TO REPENT & BE BAPTIZED...

Acts 2:38-39
Peter said to them, "Repent, and let every one of you be baptized in the name of Jesus Christ for the remission of sins; and you shall receive the gift of the Holy Spirit. For the promise is to you and to your children, and to all who are afar off, as many as the Lord our God will call.

TIMES OF REFRESHING...

Acts 3:19
Repent therefore and be converted, that your sins may be blotted out, so that times of refreshing may come from the presence of the Lord.

PRAY

LORD, I BELIEVE YOU ARE THE CREATOR AND SAVIOR OF THE WORLD. I BELIEVE YOU WANT TO SAVE AND RESCUE ME FROM SIN, HELL, AND DEATH. I KNOW I CANNOT SAVE MYSELF. PLEASE FORGIVE ME OF ALL MY SINS. POUR OUT YOUR GRACE ON MY LIFE. LORD, PLEASE HELP ME TO FORGIVE EVERYONE WHO HAS EVER WRONGED ME IN ANY WAY. TODAY, WITH YOUR HELP, I PUT THEM IN YOUR HANDS. PLEASE COME INTO MY HEART, SAVE ME, HEAL ME INSIDE AND OUT; MAKE ME A NEW CREATION. I GIVE YOU ALL OF ME, AND I WANT ALL OF YOU. FILL ME WITH YOUR HOLY SPIRIT, AND TEACH ME YOUR WAYS. HELP ME TO BECOME WHO YOU CREATED ME TO BE. IN THE NAME OF THE LORD JESUS CHRIST, AMEN

SALVATION IS A GIFT!

Eph 2:8
By grace you have been saved through faith, and that not of yourselves; it is the gift of God, not of works, lest anyone should boast.

YOU ARE A NEW CREATION!

2 Corinthians 5:17
If anyone is in Christ, he is a new creation; old things have passed away; behold, all things have become new.

ANGELS CELEBRATE!

Luke 15:10
I say to you, there is joy in the presence of the angels of God over one sinner who repents.

NO CONDEMNATION!

Romans 8:1
So now there is no condemnation for those who belong to Christ Jesus.

GOD WILL TURN IT AROUND!

Romans 8:28
We know that God causes everything to work together for the good of those who love God and are called according to his purpose for them.

GET UP!

Proverbs 24:16
A righteous man falls seven times, and rises again, But the wicked stumble in time of disaster and collapse.

GO!

Matthew 28:19
Go therefore and make disciples of all the nations, baptizing them in the name of the Father and of the Son and of the Holy Spirit.

TRUST!

Prov 3:5-6
Trust in the Lord with all your heart, and lean not on your own understanding; in all your ways acknowledge Him and He shall direct your paths.

IF you prayed to accept Jesus for the first time, or just rededicated your heart to Him, YOU DID AWESOME! Grab your smart phone and download the YouVersion Bible app. Start by listening to the book of John, then Genesis. The Bible is spiritual food for your soul. PRAYERFULLY find a good Bible believing, Bible teaching church. Get baptized, and pray every day. Keep God first no matter what.

Email us about your faith in Jesus.

GraceFellowship@live.com

GraceFellowship.info
LIVE LIFE TO GIVE LIFE

Made in the USA
Middletown, DE
30 October 2023

41529187R00018